THE EPISTLᴇꜱ ᴏꜰ JESUS CHRIST and ABGARUS KING of EDESSA

GORE COMMENTARRIES

Volume 6

Dedication

This book is dedicated to my Sister Julia…
Love you sis!

Purpose of this Book

The Purpose of this book is to enlighten those who have questions that need answers that cannot be found in the Holy Bible. This work is in NO! Way suggesting that the bible is incomplete in fact these Scriptures will show you that the Bible is complete and lacks nothing. Furthermore this work is designed for the serious Biblical Student who is searching for the story between the lines; this work is an invaluable guide to help cross reference and to develop a complete understanding of the scripture. I pray to our Lord Jesus Christ that your eyes will be open your ears will hear His Spirit & that you will become a far greater teacher, student, faithful believer than before you undertook this journey. I also pray that you will enjoy your journey may our Lord bless you. Amen.

Origination of this Textual Scripture &

History of this Gospel

The scripture states in verse one chapter one that it is a letter written to Jesus of Nazareth who the writer calls "Saviour" from ABGARUS, king of Edessa who reigned from 13-50 AD. This fact is actually widely accepted by all Christian Historians! This scripture has passed every test mankind could throw at it "carbon dating" paper and ink, even penmanship! And has been certified by the best in the world as authentic! There has been a long running attempt to have this epistle entered into the cannon but to date that has not happened.

Eusebius the Bishop of Caesarea, who lived in Palestine, in the early part of the fourth century found their genuineness, he searched the public registers and records of the City of Edessa in Mesopotamia, where Abgarus reigned, affirms that he found them written, in the Syriac language. Written by the king's hand and the reply written in the Lord Jesus Christ hand!!!

Archbishop Cave & Doctor Parker, and a gentleman named Grabe and other religious leaders have strenuously contended for their admission into the canon of Scripture as the Holy Bible is a Religious collection. The Epistle of Jesus Christ and Abgarus King of Edessa are deemed apocryphal meaning hidden.

It was said that Reverent Jeremiah Jones stated that "the people in England have this Epistle in their houses, in many places, fixed in a frame, with the picture of Christ before it; and that they generally, with much honesty and devotion, regard it as the word of God, and the genuine Epistle of Christ."

Authenticity of Text

Authenticity is without doubt as both letters are recorded in the king's records and copies have actually never been fully out of Christian hands since it was written making this piece possibly the most authentic of all known Christian literature!

The first chapter is written by King Abgarus & the second by Jesus Christ himself.

Biblical Fact on the Holy Bible

The first fact to learn about the Bible is that the Bible is not a Book it is in fact a "Collection" of works!

The word Bible means "Paper" So we have Holy for the word "Scripture" and the word Bible for the word "Paper so the Holy Bible could be called "Scripture Paper" simply meaning Scripture Written on Paper!

Now what did this tell anyone firstly that it's Scripture and all Scripture is HOLY!

Secondly it tells us what material it has been recorded on as paper was used commonly in the middle ages but in Christ time it was Scrolls made of Papyrus since the time of Moses Papyrus is a thick poor quality paper-like material produced from the pith of the papyrus plant, Cyperus papyrus, a wetland sedge that was once abundant in the Nile Delta of Egypt.

Picture of Papyrus plant growing on the river banks of the Nile River.

It is interesting that the Holy Bible could have easily had a different name!

a.   Holy Bible

b.   Scripture Paper

c.   Scripture Papyrus

d.   Scripture Scrolls

Picture of Paper Scrolls of Scripture.

Each Old Testament book was originally a book or a Series of Religious records written on Scrolls & the New Testament books were of Letters all by themselves!

All the individual letters you can still see the breakup of the letters they are your chapter breaks! They have been compiled over time and put back together but some Canonical Gospels do have some missing Chapter which have been found but due to Stubbornness of blinded Christians have yet to be added back into their rightful place. This is a fact that should put us all to shame!

In fact several New Testament Books were letters of monologue of communication between the Church and the Apostles which have been gathered together for us to read today.

Un-fortunately according to the Western Christian Church's traditional teachings, we only have the Apostles replies, as to date the church claims that no church letters to the Apostles have been found, which leads us to believe that they have not survived the test of time, however from time to time missing manuscript turn up!

In fact many of the letters have now been found and collected, but the church still denies there existence even after holding copies for several centuries they still officially teach that non have survived.

I myself have several copies of church letters to the Apostles and many other Gospels who have befallen the same ignorance, which you will find in some of my later works! Until then I dare not show them! As this work is my only avenue to protect and distribute them! And this is not un-common in fact and the Bible is not the only one to befall this same tribulation in late 2011.

A Royal Seals was found in Victoria, Australia sitting in a shed! Found in a scrap iron pile, it had been used for decades as a door stop... no-one was aware of the priceless artefact that was estimated to be worth several million dollars.

It most likely comes as a great surprise to hear that many of the books that are contained in the Bible are somewhat disputed as we have many different examples, in fact an exhaustive search of world Christian/ Catholic denominations found a remarkable finding.

After searching the "Weston Traditions", Protestant & Roman Catholic, "Eastern Orthodox Traditions", Greek Orthodox, Slavonic Orthodox, Coptic Orthodox, Ethiopian Orthodox, "Assyrian Eastern Tradition", Assyrian Church of the East, Coptic Gnostic churches.

The following was found that not a single Bible from any Denomination had or has the exact same books... In fact many Cannon and Non-Cannon books were in dispute.

Most Protestant bibles had 66 books, most Catholic 88 books and the oldest Pentecostal denomination had 91 books, the Jewish bible 24 books and all claim their version is the right one and the only complete one!

It should be taught in all seminaries that the warning of Revelations 22:19 only can be held to the book of Revelations and no other to do so is an error of Biblical Translation and misleading.

Rev 22:19 If anyone takes away any words from this book of prophecy, God will take away his portion of the tree of life and the holy city that are described in this book.

One must collect and discern according to scripture… I put it this way! If it conflicts with the Holy Bible through it out! If it up lifts the Holy Bible and clarifies then hold it dear to your heart for you may have found scripture.

CHAPTER 1

A copy of a letter written by King Abgarus to Jesus, and sent to him by Ananias, his footman, to Jerusalem, 5 inviting him to Edessa.

ABGARUS, king of Edessa, to Jesus the good Saviour, who appears at Jerusalem, greeting.

2 I have been informed concerning you and your cures, which are performed without the use of medicines and herbs.

3 For it is reported, that you cause the blind to see, the lame to walk, do both cleanse lepers, and cast out unclean spirits and devils, and restore them to health who have been long diseased, and raised up the dead;

4 All which when I heard, I was persuaded of one of these two, forces either that you are God himself descended from heaven, who do these things, or the son of God.

5 On this account therefore I have wrote to you, earnestly to desire you would take the trouble of a journey here, and cure a disease which I am under.

6 For I hear the Jews ridicule you, and intend you mischief.

7 My city is indeed small, but neat, and large enough for us both.

Commentary Chapter 1

V1 –

As stated this letter is a COPY of the original. It is not known what happened to the original sent to Jesus or the reply sent to King Abgarus from Jesus which was delivered by Ananias.

Intruction to the three people as mentioned:

ABGARUS, king of Edessa: was king from AD 13–50 was according to historical records a Syriac ruler of the kingdom of Osrhoene, holding his capital at Edessa.

This region was referred to as Armenian Mesopotamia by the Greeks and Ashur in the Old Testament.

According to an ancient legend, he was converted to Christianity by Addai, also known as Thaddeus one of the Seventy-two Disciples.

A Picture of ABGARUS, king of Edessa that
was created in the 1880's.

Ananias also known as Thaddeus and in a Syriac-Aramaic translation as Addai or Aday in Latin as Addeus:

Who was one of the Seventy Apostles of Christ, not to be confused with Thaddeus (Jude the Apostle) of the Twelve Apostles.

We do not know the age or when Ananias was born but we do know that he was a Jew born in Edessa, at the time a Syrian city, today that city is in modern Turkey. He came to Jerusalem for a festival no doubt that this was the harvest festival.

Ananias heard the preachings of John the Baptist the son of Elizabeth & Zacharias the high priest who King Herod had murdered in the temple as he thought the priest was the father of the Messiah! John the Baptist was the cousin of Jesus of Nazareth.

Ananias remained with John the Baptist after being baptized by John the Baptist in the Jordan River, he remained in Palestine. He later met and became a follower of Jesus after the beheading of John the Baptist. He was chosen to be one of the Seventy Disciples, whom Jesus sent in pairs to preach in the cities and places.

Picture of Ananias or Thaddeus 10th century,
Saint Catherine's Monastery, Mount Sinai.

V2 –

King Abgarus had obviously heard of the stories from the many visitors he received in his palace. It is here the King points out that these healing miracles are performed without any medicines or herbs which were the method of traditional healers in the land! This is still the same as today our doctor's cure with Medicines and our Naturopaths heal with herbs.

V3 –

A marvellous witness of the events that prove exactly what has been reported in the Gospels and several other Lost & Forgotten Scriptures. See Matthew 4:23.

    a. **For it is reported, that** – So here we have proof that word was indeed traveling about the miracles of Jesus of Nazareth. See Matthew 9:26; Matthew 4:24; 14:1-2; Mark 1:45; 6:14; Acts 26:26.

    b. **You cause the blind to see** – Here the King Abgarus gives complete credit to Jesus for healing the blind. See

Matthew 9:27-30; 20:34; John 9:6-7; Mark 10:46-52; Isaiah 43:8.

c. **The lame to walk** – King Abgarus gives complete credit to Jesus for the healing of the lame making the lame not only able to walk but also able to resume life in the economic social order through the ability to earn an income once again. See Matthew 15:30-31; 21:14; Acts 3:2-8; Acts 14:8-10.

d. **Do both cleanse lepers** – King Agbarus gives complete credit to Jesus for healing Leapers which was and still is a terrible disease. See Mark 1:39, Matthew 8:2-4; 11:5; Luke 5:12-14; 17:12-19; Leviticus 13:1-14:57; Numbers 12:10-15; Deuteronomy 24:8-9; 2 Samuel 3:29; 2 Kings 5:5-27; 5:27; 7:3; 15:5; The first Gospel of the Infancy of Jesus Christ 6:16-19; 6:20-36; 12:1-22.

e. **Cast out unclean spirits and devils** - King Agbarus gives Jesus complete credit for casting out unclean spirits and devils (demons) proof outside of the Gospel canon that Jesus Christ held and has power over all the demonic forces including power over Satan! See Matthew 12:22-23; Mark

9:17-27; Luke 11:14; The first Gospel of the Infancy of Jesus Christ 4:14-17; 6:1-6; 6:5-10; 6: 11-15; 7:5-27; 13:14-20.

f. **Restore them to health who have been long diseased** – King Agbarus gives credit to Jesus for healing the long term ill. With healings like the woman who had the long term issue of blood flow. See Matthew 9:20; 15:28; Mark 1:40, The first Gospel of the Infancy of Jesus Christ 7:1-4; 9; 10:1-3, 13:1-13; 14:1-10.

g. **Raised up the dead** – Jesus had raised many from the dead however in the Holy Bible there is only one recorded account but many in the lost gospels. See Matthew 9:24-25; Luke 7:14-16; Luke 7:22; John 11:43-44; Thomas the Israelite Philosopher's Account of the Infancy of the Lord 13:1-6; 14:1-4.

V4 –

King Agbarus by confession here becomes a believer and is also listed amongst the 70 disciples. It is right here that Agbarus believes that Jesus is either God in the flesh on earth or a heavenly angel.

V5 –

King Agbarus invites Jesus to come to his city stating that he was suffering a disease and in need of a cure! The disease is not named.

V6 –

Word in the cities was indeed out! News had spread far and wide of the spite full intent of the Jewish religious leaders to rid themselves of Jesus for they not only mocked and ridiculed Him for they were also planning to take his life.

V7 –

King Agbarus does the amazing! He offers his city his kingdom to share with Jesus.

CHAPTER 2

The answer of Jesus by Ananias the footman to Abgarus the king, 3 *declining to visit Edessa.*

ABGARUS, you are happy, forasmuch as you have believed on me, whom you have not seen.

2 For it is written concerning me, that those who have seen me should not believe on me, that they who have not seen might believe and live.

3 As to that part of your letter, which relates to my giving you a visit, I must inform you, that I must fulfil all the ends of my mission in this country, and after that be received up again to him who sent me.

4 But after my ascension I will send one of my disciples, who will cure your disease, and give life to you, and all that are with you.

Commentary Chapter 2

V1 –

After Jesus had read the letter from King Abgarus that was delivered by Ananias, one of the 70 apostles who had obviously been dispatched to evangelise the kingdom of Osrhoene and the same person who later baptized Paul.

He was the bishop of Damascus. He became a martyr by being stoned in Eleutheropolis. Reference to in Acts 9:10-17; 22:12.

Jesus commends the King for his faith that could only have been revealed to the king via the Holy Spirit for the King believed that he was and is God in person. Faith without seeing that is the bases of a strong faith.

See 1 John 5:1; 5:11-14; 3:16; Romans 3:22.

V2 –

Jesus commends the King for his extraordinary faith in Him even though the King had never met Jesus.

See 2 Corinthians 5:7; Romans 8:24-25; Hebrews 11:1-26.

V3 –

Jesus sadly tells the king that he is unable to visit. We do know that this letter came to Jesus in the last 6 months of His ministry before the cross and here points out that he was to be raised up by the one who sent him… God the Father!

V4 –

   a. But after my ascension – After Jesus has died on the cross and risen on the third day!
   b. I will send one of my disciples – This could of possible happened at Pentecost in the room.
   c. Who will cure your disease – Jesus had faith in the faith of His believers even if they had little faith in themselves.
   d. And give life to you – Life, belief in forgiveness of sins.
   e. And all that are with you – This same word or Gospel was to be preached to all the kings subjects in the land!

The seventy apostles of Christ

The seventy apostles of Jesus of Nazareth who became known and accepted as Jesus our Christ and Risen Saviour were chosen in addition to the twelve disciples.

Their number hovered around the seventy plus, however they were always called "the seventy".

However, the names of the original seventy are unknown, as is shown in the Gospel of John: "...many of His disciples went back, and walked with Him no more. Then said Jesus to the Twelve, Do you also want to go away?" John 6:66-67.

As you read the two main lists below no doubt you will recognize many names! Both for their faithfulness, works and achievements.

The names included in both lists differ slightly. In the lists, Luke is also one of these seventy himself.

The following list gives a widely accepted canon. Their names are listed below; along with the where in the Holy Bible it can be viewed:

List One of the Seventy

1.	James "the Lord's brother" also called James the Just, author of the Epistle of James, and first Bishop of Jerusalem however this may have been a shared role. As sometimes is replaced by Jacob Joses Justus, who was also a brother of Jesus, since James the Just is identified as one of the twelve apostles in Matthew 13:55; Mark 6:3, Acts 12:17, 15:13; Epistle of James.

2.	Agabus. Acts 11:28; 21:10.

3.	Amplias. Romans 16:8.

4.	Mark the Evangelist, author of the Gospel of Mark and Bishop of Alexandria.

5.	Luke the Evangelist, author of the Gospel of Luke.

6.	Cleopas.

7.   Simeon, son of Cleopas, 2nd Bishop of Jerusalem.

8.   Barnabas, companion of the Apostle Paul.

9.   Justus, Bishop of Eleutheropolis.

10.   Thaddeus of Edessa not the Apostle called Thaddeus also known as Saint Addai; Ananias, Bishop of Damascus.

11.   Stephen, one of the Seven Deacons, the first martyr in the New Testament after the crucifixion of Jesus.

12.   Philip the Evangelist, one of the Seven Deacons, Bishop of Tralles in Asia Minor.

13.   Prochorus, one of the Seven Deacons, Bishop of Nicomedia in Bithynia.

14.   Nicanor the Deacon, one of the Seven Deacons.

15.   Timon, one of the Seven Deacons.

16.   Parmenas the Deacon, one of the Seven Deacons.

17.   Timothy, Bishop of Ephesus.

18.   Titus, Bishop of Crete.

19.   Philemon, Bishop of Gaza.

20.   Onesimus not the Onesimus mentioned in the Epistle to Philemon.

21.   Epaphras, Bishop of Andriaca.

22.   Archippus.

23.   Silas, Bishop of Corinth.

24.   Silvanus.

25.   Crescens.

26.   Crispus, Bishop of Chalcedon in Galilee.

27.   Epenetus, Bishop of Carthage.

28.   Andronicus, Bishop of Pannonia.

29.   Stachys, Bishop of Byzantium.

30. Amplias, Bishop of Odissa (Odessus).

31. Urban, Bishop of Macedonia.

32. Narcissus, Bishop of Athens.

33. Apelles, Bishop of Heraklion.

34. Aristobulus, Bishop of Britain.

35. Herodion, Bishop of Patras.

36. Agabus the Prophet.

37. Rufus, Bishop of Thebes.

38. Asyncritus, Bishop of Hyrcania.

39. Phlegon, Bishop of Marathon.

40. Hermes, Bishop of Philippopolis.

41. Parrobus, Bishop of Pottole.

42. Hermas, Bishop of Dalmatia.

43. Pope Linus, Bishop of Rome.

44. Gaius, Bishop of Ephesus.

45. Philologus, Bishop of Sinope.

46. Lucius of Cyrene, Bishop of Laodicea in Syria.

47. Jason, Bishop of Tarsus.

48. Sosipater, Bishop of Iconium.

49. Olympas.

50. Tertius, transcriber of the Epistle to the Romans and Bishop of Iconium.

51. Erastus, Bishop of Paneas.

52. Quartus, Bishop of Berytus.

53. Euodias, Bishop of Antioch.

54. Onesiphorus, Bishop of Cyrene.

55. Clement, Bishop of Sardis.

56. Sosthenes, Bishop of Colophon.

57. Apollos, Bishop of Caesarea.

58. Tychicus, Bishop of Colophon.

59. Epaphroditus.

60. Carpus, Bishop of Beroea in Thrace.

61.   Quadratus.

62.   John Mark bishop of Byblos.

63.   Zenas the Lawyer, Bishop of Diospolis.

64.   Aristarchus, Bishop of Apamea in Syria.

65.   Pudens.

66.   Trophimus.

67.   Mark, Bishop of Apollonia.

68.   Artemas, Bishop of Lystra.

69.   Aquila.

70.   Fortunatus.

71.   Achaicus 1 Corinthians 16:17.

72.   Tabitha, a woman disciple, whom Peter raised from the dead.

☐

List Two of the Seventy Apostles

1.   Archaicus. Reference to in 1 Corinthians 16:17.

2.   Agabus. Reference to in Acts 11:28; 21:10.

3.   Amplias, appointed by St. Andrew as bishop of Lydda of Odyssopolis (Diospolis) in Judea. He died a martyr. Reference to in Romans 16:8.

4.   Ananias, who baptized St. Paul. He was the bishop of Damascus. He became a martyr by being stoned in Eleutheropolis. Reference to in Acts 9:10-17; 22:12. Andronicus, bishop of Pannonia. Reference to in Romans 16:17.

5.   Apelles, bishop of Heraclea (in Trachis). Reference to in Romans 16:10.

6.   Apollos. He was a bishop of several places over time: Crete, Corinth, Smyrna, and Caesarea. Reference to in Acts 18:24;

19:1; 1 Corinthians 1:12; 3:4-22; 4:6; 16:12, Titus 3:13.

7.   Aquila. He was martyred. Reference to in Acts 18:2, 18, 26; Romans 16:3; 1 Corinthians 16:19; 2 Timothy 4:19.

8.   Archippus. Reference to in Colossians 4:17; Philemon 2.

9.   Aristarchus, bishop of Apamea in Syria. He was martyred under Nero. "Aristarchus, whom Paul mentions several times, calling him a 'fellow labourer,' became bishop of Apamea in Syria." Orthodox Study Bible Reference to in Acts 19:29; 20:4; 27:2; Colossians 4:10; Philemon 24.

10.   Aristobulus, bishop of Britain. "...the brother of the apostle Barnabas, preached the gospel in Great Britain and died peacefully there." Orthodox Study Bible Reference to in Romans 16:14.

11.   Artemas, bishop of Lystra in Lycia. Reference to in Titus 3:12.

12.   Aristarchus, bishop of Hyracania in Asia. Reference to in Romans 16:14.

13.   Barnabas. "A Jew of the Tribe of Levi, was born in Cyprus of wealthy parents. He is said to have studied under Gamaliel with Saul of Tarsus, who was to become Paul the apostle. Originally named Joseph, he was called Barnabas (Son of Consolation) by the apostles because he had a rare gift of comforting people's hearts. He sought out Paul when everyone else was afraid of him, bringing him to the apostles. It was Barnabas whom the apostles first sent to Antioch with Paul. Their long association was broken only when Barnabas was determined to take his cousin Mark, whom Paul did not trust just then, on a missionary journey. The three were later reconciled. Many ancient accounts say Barnabas was the first to preach in Rome and in Milan, but he was martyred in Cyprus, then buried by Mark at the western gate of the city of Salamis." Orthodox Study Bible Reference to in Acts

4:36; 9:27; 11-15; 1 Corinthians 9:6; Galatians 2:1,9,13; Colossians 4:10.

14. Caesar, bishop of Dyrrhachium (in the Peloponnese of Greece).

15. Carpus, bishop of Berroia (Verria, in Macedonia. Reference to in 2 Timothy 4:13.

16. Clement, bishop in Sardis. Reference to in Philippians 4:3.

17. Cephas, bishop of Iconium, Pamphyllia.

18. Cleopas, was with the Lord on the road to Emmaus. Reference to in Luke 24:18; John 19:25.

19. Crescens, later bishop of Galatia. He was martyred under the Emperor Trajan. Reference to in 2 Timothy 4:10.

20. Crispus, bishop of Aegina, Greece. Reference to in Acts 18:8; 1 Corinthians 1:14.

21. Epaphras. Reference to in Colossians 1:7; 4:12; Philemon 23.

22.   Epaphroditus, bishop of the Thracian city of Adriaca. Reference to in Philippians 2:25; 4:18.

23.   Epaenetus, bishop of Carthage. Reference to in Romans 16:5.

24.   Erastus. He served as a deacon and steward to the Church of Jerusalem. Later he served in Palestine. Reference to in Acts 19:22; Romans 16:23; 2 Timothy 4:20.

25.   Euodias (Evodius), first bishop of Antioch after St.Peter. He wrote several compositions. At the age of sixty-six, under the Emperor Nero, he was martyred. Reference to in Philippians 4:2.

26.   Fortunatus. Reference to in 1 Corinthians 16:17.

27.   Gaius, bishop of Ephesus. Reference to in Acts 19:29; 20:4; Romans 16:23; 1 Corinthians 1:14; 3 John 1.

28.   Hermas, bishop in Philipopoulis. He wrote The Shepherd of Hermas. he

died a martyr. Reference to in Romans 16:14.

29.   Hermes, bishop of Dalmatia. Reference to in Romans 16:14.

30.   Herodion, a relative of the Apostle Paul, bishop of Neoparthia. He was beheaded in Rome. Reference to in Romans 16:11.

31.   James, brother of the Lord(also called "the Less" or "the Just"). He was a (step-)brother to Jesus, by Jesus' Father Joseph, through a previous marriage. James was the Patriarch of Jerusalem. Reference to in Matthew 13:55; Mark 6:3; Acts 12:17; 15:13; Epistle of James.

32.   Jason, bishop of Tarsus. Traveling with Sosipater to Corfu, the two were able, after an attempt made at their lives by the king of Corfu, to convert his majesty. Reference to in Acts 17:5-9.

33.   Justus, brother to the Lord and bishop of Eleutheropolis. He was the half-brother of Christ(as was Sts. James, Jude,

and Simon) through Joseph's previous marriage to Salome. He died a martyr. Reference to in Acts 1:23; 18:7; Colossians 4:11.

34.   Linus, bishop of Rome. Reference to in 2 Timothy 4:21.

35.   Lucius, bishop of Laodicea. Reference to in Acts 13:1; Romans 16:21.

36.   Luke the Evangelist. He is the author of the Gospel of Luke, and the founder of Iconography (Orthodox Icon-writing). Reference to in Colossians 4:14; 2 Timothy 4:11; Philemon 24.

37.   Mark the Evangelist (called John). He wrote the Gospel of Mark. He also founded the Church of Alexandria, serving as its first bishop. Reference to in Acts 12:12, 25; 15:37-39; Colossians 4:10; 2 Timothy 4:11; Philemon 24; 1 Peter 5:13.

38.   Mark.

39.   Narcissus, ordained by the Apostle Philip as bishop of Athens, Greece. Reference to in Romans 16:11.

40.   Nicanor, one of the original seven deacons. He was martyred on the same day as the Promartyr Stephen. Reference to in Acts 6:5.

41.   Olympas, beheaded with St. Peter under Nero. Reference to in Romans 16:15.

42.   Onesimus. Onesimus preached the Gospel in many cities. He was made bishop of Ephesus, and later bishop of Byzantium (Constantinople). He was martyred under the Emperor Trajan. Reference to in Colossians 4:9; Philemon 10.

43.   Onesiphorus, bishop of Colophon (Asia Minor), and later of Corinth. He died a martyr in Parium. Reference to in 2 Timothy 1:16; 4:19.

44.   Parmenas, one of the original seven deacons. He preached throughout Asia Minor, and later settled in Macedonia. He was a bishop of Soli. He died a martyr in Macedonia. Reference to in Acts 6:5.

45.   Patrobus, bishop of Neapolis (Naples). Reference to in Romans 16:14.

46.   Philemon. He, with his wife Apphia, and the apostle Archippus, were martyred by pagans during a pagan feast. Reference to in Philemon 1.

47.   Philip the Deacon (one of the original seven). He was born in Palestine, and later preached throughout its adjoining lands. In Acts, he converts a eunuch (an official) of Candace, queen of Ethiopia, to Christ. He was later made bishop by the apostles at Jerusalem, who also sent him to Asia Minor. Reference to in Acts 6; 8; 21:8.

48.   Philologus, ordained bishop of Sinope (near the Black sea) by the Apostle Andrew. Reference to in Romans 16:15.

49.   Phlegon, bishop of Marathon, in Thrace. Reference to in Romans 16:14.

50.   Prochorus, one of the original seven deacons. He was made bishop of Nicomedia by St. Peter. He was later

banished with the Apostle John (John the Theologian) to the Island of Patmos. In Antioch, he died a martyr. Reference to in Acts 6:5.

51.   Pudens (Pastorum). He was an esteemed member of the Roman Senate, then received Sts. Peter and Paul into his home, and was converted to Christ by them. He was martyred under Nero. Reference to in Acts 6:5.

52.   Quadratus, bishop of Athens. He was author of the Apologia. He was stoned, but survived. Soon-after, he died of starvation in prison.

53.   Quartus, bishop of Beirut. Reference to in Romans 16:23.

54.   Rufus, bishop of Thebes, Greece. Reference to in Mark 15:21; Romans 16:13.

55.   Silas (Silvanus), bishop of Corinth. Reference to in Acts 15:22-40; 16:19-40; 17:4-15; 18:5; 2 Corinthians 1:19; 1

Thessalonians 1:1; 2 Thessalonians 1:1; 1 Peter 5:12.

56.   Simeon, son of Cleopas. "Simeon, son of Cleopas (who was the brother of Joseph, the betrothed of the Virgin Mary), succeeded James as bishop of Jerusalem." Orthodox Study Bible He was martyred through torture and crucifixion, at the age of one-hundred. Reference to in Matthew 13:55; Mark 6:3.

57.   Sosipater, ordained bishop of Iconium by the Apostle Paul, his relative. With St. Jason, he converted the king of Corfu. Reference to in Romans 16:21.

58.   Sosthenes. "...became bishop of Caesarea." Orthodox Study Bible Reference to in 1 Corinthians 1:1.

59.   Stachys, ordained by St. Andrew to be bishop of Byzantium. Reference to in Romans 16:9.

60.   Stephen the Promartyr and Archdeacon (one of the original seven

deacons). Reference to in Acts 6:5-7:60; 8:2 (Acts 6:5-8:2); 11:19; 22:20.

61.   Tertius, bishop of Iconium (after Sosipater). He wrote down St. Paul's letter to the Romans. He died a martyr. Reference to in Romans 16:22.

62.   Thaddaeus. He was baptized by John the Baptist (John the Forerunner). He later preached, and founded a Church in Beirut. Reference to in Matthew 10:3; Mark 3:18.

63.   Timon,one of the original seven deacons, and later bishop of Bostra (in Arabia). He was thrown into a furnace, but emerged unharmed. Reference to in Acts 6:5.

64.   Timothy. He accompanied St. Paul often, and both 1 and 2 Timothy are addressed to him. He was ordained bishop of Ephesus by St. Paul. He died a martyr. Reference to in Acts 16:1; 17:14, 15; 18:5; 19:22; 20:4; Romans 16:21; 1 and 2 Timothy.

65.   Titus. " Among the more prominent of the seventy was the apostle Titus, whom Paul called his brother and his son. Born in Crete, Titus was educated in Greek philosophy, but after reading the prophet Isaiah he began to doubt the value of all he had been taught. Hearing the news of the coming of Jesus Christ, he joined some others from Crete who were going to Jerusalem to see for themselves. After hearing Jesus speak and seeing His works, the young Titus joined those who followed Him. Baptized by the apostle Paul, he worked with and served the great apostle of the gentiles, traveling with him until Paul sent him to Crete, making him bishop of that city. It is said that Titus was in Rome at the time of the beheading of St. Paul and that he buried the body of his spiritual father before returning home. Back in Crete, he converted and baptized many people, governing the Church on that island until he entered into rest at the age of ninety-four." Orthodox Study Bible Reference to in 2 Corinthians 2:13; 7:6-14; 8:6-23; 12:18; Galatians 2:1-3; Epistle to Titus.

66.   Trophimus, disciple of St.Paul, and martyred under Nero. Reference to in Acts 20:4; 21:29; 2 Timothy 4:20.

67.   Tychicus. "succeeded him (Sosthenes, as bishop) in that city (of Caesarea)." Orthodox Study Bible He delivered St. Paul's letter to the Ephesians and Colossians. Reference to in Acts 20:4; Ephesians 6:21; Colossians 4:7; 2 Timothy 4:12; Titus 3:12.

68.   Urbanus, ordained by the Apostle Andrew as bishop of Macedonia. He died a martyr. Reference to in Romans 16:9.

69.   Zenas, (called 'the lawyer') bishop of Diospolis (Lydda), in Palestine Reference to in Titus 3:13.

70.   Alphaeus, father of the apostle James and Matthew.

71.   Apphia, wife to the Apostle Philemon. The Church had gathered in her home for liturgy, while pagans who had been celebrating a pagan feast broke in and raided her home. They took

Apphia, Philemon, and Archippus to be killed. She suffered martyrdom, and is commemorated by the Church on February 19.

72.   Junia, accompanied Andronicus in preaching all over Pannonia. She was a relative to the Apostle Paul, and a martyr.

73.   Silvan, bishop of Thessaloniki, Greece. Reference to in 1 Peter 5:12; 2 Corinthians 1:19.

74.   Zacchaeus, appointed by St.Peter to be bishop of Caesarea. Reference to in Luke 19:1-10.

Reference:

- Ref: http://www.babycentre.co.uk/

- Reference: http://www.livius.org/he-hg/herodians/herod_antipas.html

- References: If not directly stated I have lost or miss placed... All evidence & quotes, material and pictures sourced through the internet and authorship was unknown.

- Cover Picture taken by Ian Donaldson of The Titus Arch in Rome that celebrates the destruction of the Temple in 70 AD by Titus as Matthew 24 prophesied, however we know that no artefacts were removed by Titus and his men as the temple caught fire and burnt down.

- Internet Sacred Text Achieve

- Missing Books of the Bible– where are they? by James Denison, Ph.D. ,

Senior Pastor of Park Cities Baptist Church, Dallas, Texas

• Excerpted from: Denison, James C. "The Real Painter of the Gospel: The Da Vinci Code in the Light of History" Feb 2006. pp 5-6

• Wikipedia

• Clark

• Webster Dictionary

• Picture: Viper Snake in twigs by, rfadventures.com

• Picture: Viper Snake ready to strike, redgage.com

• Picture: Rooftops, by unknown artist.

• Encyclopaedia Britannica

• Spikenard: www.essentialoils.co.za/essential-oils/spikenard.htm

• Smith's Bible Dictionary

- Andronicus, bishop of Pannonia. Reference to in Romans 16:17.

To all those great known & unknown writers out there I thank you! Without your selfless acts this book would not be!

Lost & Forgotten Books of the New Testament□

GORE COMENTARIES

Authors Address: Pastor Michael Gore

DBS - Diploma in Biblical Studies, ADM - Associate Degree in Ministry, BTC - Bible Teachers Certificate, APD - Associate Pastor Diploma, BTH - Bachelor of Theology, M. Min - Master of Ministry

I started studying the "Lost Scriptures" a few years back. I had questions that I needed answers for that the Holy Bible did not contain, for instance I wanted to know where Jesus Christ got the material for the "Sermon on the Mount" Well I found it! I wanted to know more about the conception of Christ, Well I found it! Most of all I wanted to know why according to which Christian Denomination you belonged to had different Bibles with different books, some Bibles had as little as 24 books while others ranged all the way out to 91 books! I was no longer interested in hearing others opinions I wanted to read, study for myself, and form my own opinion on each subjective book. I wanted to see the truth at the back off it.

I hope and pray that as you read along and study with me and that you too will have a new and refreshed revelation of our Jesus Christ who in every book proves to be more magnificent than I could imagine!

First a little about myself: I am an Apostolic Pastor, over the years I have served in many different challenging positions in ministry. I have been a Church planter, Youth Pastor and my last appointment as Senior Pastor at Arise Apostolic Church in Ballarat, Victoria, Australia a small church under 30 souls.

In my private work life I have worked as a Fitter & Turner, Soldier, Welder, and Loss Prevention Investigator.

I am married to my beautiful wife Anissa, with three children and one granddaughter.

☐

Other Books by this Author

All these books may be found at amazon.com & on Kindle Books! They are purposely priced low as this is a ministry and the proceeds support training of future ministers!

Scripture & Commentary

Series: Lost & Forgotten books of the New Testament

1.   The First Gospel of the INFANCY of JESUS CHRIST

2.   Thomas's Gospel of the INFANCY of JESUS CHRIST

3.   Thomas the Israelite Philosophers Account of the Infancy of the Lord

4.   The Protevangelion of James

5.   The Gospel of the Birth of Mary

6.   The Epistle of Jesus Christ and Abgarus King of Edessa.

☐

☐

Biblical Teaching Books

1.   Christianity and the Mosaic Law

2.   Today's Relevance of the Old Law – Based on Deuteronomy 7:1-5

3.   Adequate Warning

Self-Help

1.   Runaway Teenager the first 48 Hours☐